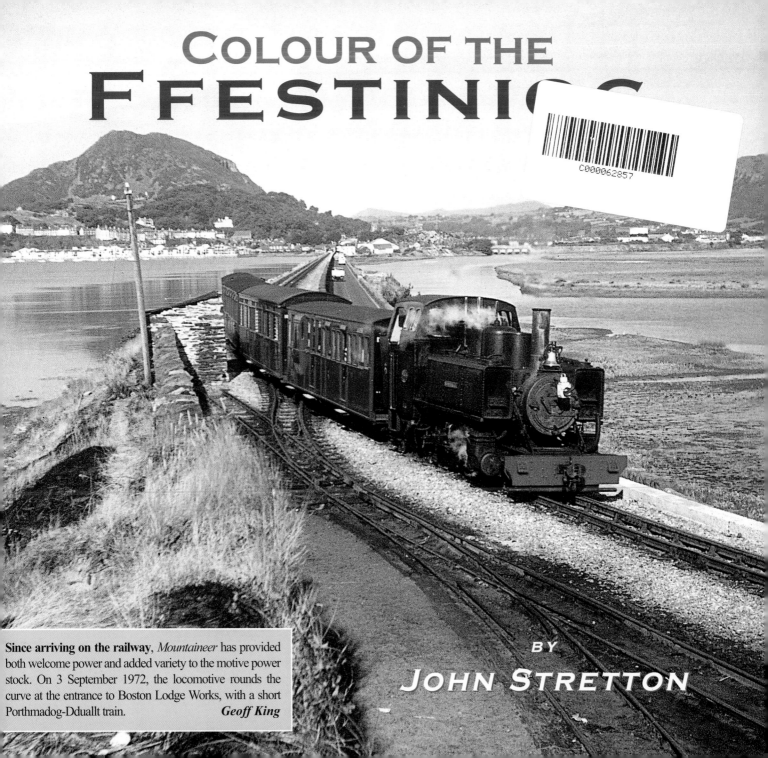

COLOUR OF THE
FFESTINIOG

Since arriving on the railway, *Mountaineer* has provided both welcome power and added variety to the motive power stock. On 3 September 1972, the locomotive rounds the curve at the entrance to Boston Lodge Works, with a short Porthmadog-Dduallt train.
Geoff King

BY
JOHN STRETTON

ISBN 1 870119 70 3

Designed by Foxline (Publications) Ltd
P O Box 84 BREDBURY SK6 3YD

Printed by the Amadeus Press, Cleckheaton, West Yorkshire.

DEDICATION

This book is respectfully and affectionately dedicated to **Leonard (Len) Heath-Humphrys,** who died suddenly during its preparation, shortly before Christmas 2000. Had it not been for his initiative of writing to the press about the FR in 1951, it is quite conceivable that the railway as we know it today would not have existed and so many people would not have had such immense pleasure from it. I found him an interesting companion and always willing to help - ever the gentleman. He will be greatly missed.

ACKNOWLEDGEMENTS

During the many hours and months that have seen the gestation and production of this book, there have been numerous people who have contributed. Some have given much, others less so, but each in their own way has added to the whole and the result would have been the poorer without them; they all know who they are. I have been constantly amazed at the wealth of material available and each packet arriving in the post has generated much excitement and real pleasure, especially where material has arrived unsolicited. Space precludes listing everyone, but amongst those who have given of their time, advice, thoughts and work, there are those who deserve especial mention. Thanks therefore go, in no particular order of merit, to the 'gang of four' - Richard Hanlon, Adrian Gray, Peter Jarvis and Andy Savage - who in their proof-reading have pointed this relative ignoramus along (hopefully!) the right track; Hugh Ballantyne; David Johnson of Millbrook House; Gerald Adams; Dick Riley and Michael Mensing (especially for their collective patience!); Roy Wakeford; Eric Bareham; Howard Wilson; Bryan Hicks; Geoff King; Albert Sell (for pointing his camera where others 'feared to tread'!); Tom Heavyside; Kevin Heywood; Roy Needler; and Peter Treloar (for being so trusting and ever helpful). Foxline deserves a huge bouquet for sharing something of my vision and having the will to proceed; as do my wife, Judi and daughter, Tammy, for their own involvement in the railway as volunteers and for supporting my interest. Both have appeared in the book, in differing guises and the absence of any of Tammy's photographs is absolutely no reflection on her skills as a photographer! I hope some of the pleasure I have had in preparing the book is transmitted to the reader.

Real colour, in all its garish hues, came only much later to Ffestiniog stock; in the early days of preservation, concentration was focused on running trains. Concentration of another sort is shown here, as *Prince* is the recipient of undivided attention, as he stands in plain green coat in Porthmadog Harbour station on 27 June 1956. Behind is no.11, originally an 1880-vintage van, converted in 1928/9 for accommodation. Returned to service the previous year, *Prince* was the first locomotive on the railway to have an all-steel firebox and be fitted with the then to be standard couplings, a change from the 'link & hook' fitted by the old company. He is here, however, still with those inherited from the old railway. Within a year, the plain sides of the tender would be graced with an FR garter crest. Note how the cant of the curved track in the station is exaggerated by comparison of *Prince* with coach behind and building and telegraph pole beyond. As this degree of super-elevation was unnecessary for the slow speed in the platform area, it was subsequently re-laid to a more 'relaxed' angle. *Chris Banks collection*

Coming forward two years from the above view to 1958 and *Prince* has now acquired the more permanent FR coupling, as well as being adorned with an attractive 1/4" red line and black border, applied in June 1957 at the same time as double-Fairlie *Taliesin* was similarly treated. Together with brightly polished brasswork, this makes for a much more aesthetic product. Again seen in Harbour station platform, small Birmingham no.5 is next to the engine, its matchboarded exterior recently repainted in green. The unidentified fireman finds time in 1958 to hold conversation with a visitor before heading the 3.00 p.m. 'relief', nicknamed the 'Flying Flea', up the line.

Millbrook House collection

INTRODUCTION

The Ffestiniog Railway abounds in superb photographic opportunities and throughout its near-fifty years of resurrected life, there have been thousands - if not millions!?! - of pictures taken. The earliest days saw predominantly b&w, but colour has become ever more popular, with greater latitudes in emulsions and immensely enhanced quality since the mid-Fifties. Both b&w and colour have their own unique characteristics and there are points where one most definitely scores over the other, but what colour slides or prints do have, of course, is....colour! Where liveries are concerned, this can be a vital ingredient; there have been many historians, figuratively tearing their hair out, trying to guess at the possible colour combinations of a past view with only a b&w image to help them. In this book I have attempted to show just some of the examples and changes of livery and basic colour ideas on the railway, but, in addition, my emphasis has been on the 'visual treat' and what makes the FR so special.

There is much more to the railway than mere colour. There are a myriad of things that perhaps do not reach the public eye or ear, but which have profound influence on the shape and fortunes of the railway. As well as attempting to present aesthetic images - pretty pictures! - I have also tried to include other facets of the railway's day-to-day life. Hence, there are views of volunteers, stock awaiting attention, accidents, 'behind-the-scenes' developments, special events and, of course, the service trains.

As the story unfolds, with the book progressing chronologically from the early days of restoration through to the end of the century, it will be seen that an appreciation of colour developed, along with the urge to provide the travelling public with as fulfilling as possible an experience. From the relatively utilitarian all-over green, to the 'day-glo' Funkey *Vale of Ffestiniog*, the FR has mirrored society's move away from the immediate post-war years to the multi-coloured, multi-faceted, multi-disciplined era that ended the twentieth century. The railway has never been slow to identify and react to changes in our society's habits and their resultant demands. As a leisure industry, this has been essential for survival. Gone are the heady days of young volunteers

Earlier the same day in 1958, *Taliesin*, proudly wearing 'No.3', although at the time there were only two working steam locos, waits to head the 2.30pm. service to Tan-y-Bwlch. Re-opened on 5 April 1958, the extra mileage to Tan-y-Bwlch quickly proved to be very popular as can be judged from the number of passengers aboard ex-WHR coach 23 and newly-restored Ashbury no.22. The pronounced sag in the roof line of the latter earned it the affectionate nickname of the 'banana van'! Note how scruffy no.23 looks after three years in service, compared to its neighbour. Again the red lining/black border, plus the FR emblem, serve to enhance *Taliesin's* visual impact. **Millbrook House collection**

'playing trains', succeeding against all odds. Today, the railway is nothing if not professional, but it still retains a place for the amateur and an appreciation of enthusiasm and commitment.

Selecting the images found in this book has been incredibly difficult. We all have our favourite locomotive, colour, location, etc. There have been a vast number of photographs, both slide and print, that truly have deserved a place, but have been squeezed out through a lack of space coupled to a desire to show a number of differing facets, rather than a collection of chocolate box images. So, whittling down from around 1000 originals has been a nightmare, but one born of an embarrassment of riches.

There has been no attempt to present anything approaching a history of the railway - that has been done in other places and, no doubt, will be done again - but relevant data and comment has been included with the factual in compiling the captions. I hope the reader will find much to enjoy within these pages and some views that will particularly satisfy. I also hope and trust they will forgive any perceived omissions and accept my indulgences. The images are all appropriately credited to the sometimes far-sighted photographers, with those shown as **MJS** being my own.

M JOHN STRETTON January 2001

PORTHMADOG
- HARBOUR STATION

Still at Harbour on that same day in 1958, but slightly earlier than the last view, *Taliesin* takes a breather between duties, having stocked up with coal from the wagon parked on the stub of the original wharf siding. Passengers are already on board the train for the next service, whilst in earnest conversation with fireman Jim Maxwell are two scouts - remember those days of short trousers?!? The near seven feet high wall by the toilets in the left background was lowered to roughly half its height within months of this view.   ***Millbrook House collection***

Taking a wider view of Harbour station, in 1959, the slightly cramped nature of the site can be seen, with the inherited track alignment still in situ. *Taliesin* eases up to the train to allow the fireman to effect coupling, the continuing success of services to Tan-y-Bwlch evidenced by the use of the bogie coaches rather than ancient four-wheelers. Beyond, three children watch and wait, apparently ignoring *Moelwyn* standing on the goods shed road. The original fencing is still extant, right, (a feature through to the mid-1960s), with Britannia Foundry, beyond, still open for business. ***Gerald Adams***

TAN-Y-BWLCH

The other end of the line in 1959. Having safely brought its train up the line, *Taliesin*, replenished with water, stands among the sheep-nibbled grass, waiting for the passengers to be similarly refreshed. Station Mistress Bessie Jones ran a popular tea room from her front parlour, advertised by the sign over the station house front door, left. Once the train was known to have left Portmadoc, a call on the omnibus 'phone established whether the large or small kettle should be put on to boil! The point in the foreground led to the old goods shed, extended much later to take over as a fully equipped cafe. When compared with the same scene at the end of the century, the many changes in both railway and scenery are readily apparent. *Gerald Adams*

(Above) Another view of the same scene as page 7, slightly earlier in the day, as *Prince* waits to take the first train of the day back to Porthmadog. Visitors and passengers enjoy the summer sunshine, casually strolling around the temporary terminus, visiting the cafe or merely sitting on the bench; the whole emits an air of relaxation, no frenetic timetable to be obeyed. The apparent empty state of *Prince's* tender - there only being a need for a couple of hundred-weight for the downward journey - deceived many an onlooker! *Gerald Adams*

(Right) Meanwhile, somewhere out in the country! Whilst public services terminated at Tan-y-Bwlch, the line to the north of the station 'slept', allowing interested and hardy souls to casually walk the line in comparative safety. Around 1959, to the north of Garnedd Tunnel, a lady and, presumably, her teenage son, enjoy an afternoon stroll along the trackbed. Within just a few years, with the progression of the railway towards Dduallt, this activity would be outlawed! *Millbrook House collection*

The first ten years after re-opening of the railway in 1955 was largely a period of consolidation, with the push to Tan-y-Bwlch achieved and more locomotives being added to the roster. To the general public, there was probably little sign of change and certainly the scene here in 1962, at the northern terminus, echoes that perception, with the goods shed still in original condition, together with tracks leading to it and even a couple of old slate wagons 'on show'. The bottom end points by the road underbridge had been moved to this position in the winter of 1958, since gravity trains no longer ran and the loop could therefore be shorter. Later developments would see the sidings removed, the goods shed transformed into that very welcome cafe and toilets and fencing erected to protect the public from the increasingly heavy and more frequent trains. Note the original-style lettered station name board still in situ; the end of the Observation car now in green and ivory (compared to red in the 1959 view); and *Earl of Merioneth* (renamed from *Taliesin* the previous year) looking very work weary. ***Millbrook House collection***

1962 saw the arrival of a 'foreign' locomotive to the railway. Increasing patronage and decreasing reliability of the aged Festiniog locomotives led to growing demands on the already stretched operations and it became clear that additional motive power would be required. Following the closure of Penrhyn Quarry, near Bangor, Hunslet 0-4-0ST *Linda* was brought to the railway, originally on loan. Arriving on 14 July, she was put into traffic very shortly afterwards. Then and thereafter, she has proved a very welcome addition to the stock, but on 5 September 1962 she very nearly disgraced herself, in an incident forever afterwards known as 'Linda's Leap'. Without tender, as received from Penrhyn, and double-headed with *Prince* on an up train, she left the track at Squirrel Crossing, after a flange had struck the crossing timber. Initial thoughts laid the blame on gauge difference, with her back to back wheel dimension being some 3/4" less than the FR gauge, but subsequent examinations pinpointed uneven weight distribution, making her '3-legged'. Remedial action made her more sure-footed and the problem was finally overcome when she, and sister *Blanche*, were fitted with a pony truck. This view of the scene shows the crazy angle of *Linda* and work beginning to right matters.

John Dobson

(Right) **As the years rolled by and the fame of the FR spread ever wider**, the media became more interested. This, of course, brought much welcome free advertising and the opportunity to publicise the centenary of steam on the railway in 1963, through the BBC TV cameras, was gratefully taken. At Pen Cob, just outside Boston Lodge works yard, on 29 August 1963, a cameraman takes 'fill-in' shots after Tom Davies - an old FR driver who returned to work on the railway until 1969 - had been interviewed. 'Driver' Evan Davies and 'fireman' Richard Hanlon, having prepared *Prince* to look his best, stand in the foreground, watching proceedings. Note that *Prince* now has straight frames after his 1961/2 overhaul.

(Below) **Back in harness and with problems overcome**, *Linda* was paired with *Princess*' old tender. A temporary measure until her own was ready, the arrangement made use of some rusting on the old tender to couple to a water reservoir set in place behind the driver. The rather ungainly apparatus can be seen in this view of coaching stock being brought across the Cob in August 1963.

Both: *Millbrook House collection.*

The first proper station on the route up the line from Porthmadog is Minffordd, an exchange point with the national rail network. Following re-opening of the FR on 23 July 1955, extension for passenger services to Minffordd was achieved with effect from 19 May 1956. Minffordd was and is the first crossing point on the railway, giving the opportunity of seeing more than one train in the station at one time. Seen here in 1963, *Merddin Emrys,* with the square tanks fitted when restored to traffic in April 1961 and without cab roof, drifts into the station with an early afternoon down train. Behind is observation car no.11 and newly-restored coach no.14, ex-Lynton & Barnstaple, the dimensions of which make quite a contrast with the rest of the train. Fireman David McIntosh shares a comment with his driver as they slow for the station stop.
                                                                    Millbrook House collection

At the other end of the line on a bright day in May 1965, the fruits of the railway's labours and the warm spring sunshine are enjoyed by the travelling public at Tan-y-Bwlch, while *Merddin Emrys* waits for departure time. Note the presence of the brand-new Observation Car no.100, introduced on 25 May 1965 in a novel varnish livery and giving the opportunity for 1st class travel. Still in green and ivory is no.14, whose reconstruction set the style for a series of new-built carriages required for the growing traffic. The larger size of no.100 and, just visible, no.24 (now 104) soon led to them being dubbed 'Barns'.

Roy Wakeford

13

(Above) On a delightfully sunny day in September 1966, *Blanche* stands in Tan-y-Bwlch station, ready to haul the return train to Portmadoc. Interestingly, none of the motive power or coaching stock seen here was on the railway a decade or so earlier, all having been brought in or built new since preservation. *R C Riley*

(Left) The rebirth of the FR, like so many other preserved railways that followed, was fuelled by enthusiasts. In the early days, the railway's very survival depended on volunteers; since then, many have given months, even years, to ensure its development and success. Often the work is hard, dirty, and unsung, frequently unnoticed by the travelling public, but, nevertheless, vital. In the late spring of 1965, three such hardy souls are seen hard at work in the long siding, just south of Minffordd station, unloading spoil from the goods shed at Tan-y-Bwlch. *Roy Wakeford*

Following her sister, *Linda*, from Penrhyn Quarry, *Blanche* arrived on the FR in 1963. After a short period paired with the old tender from England engine *Princess*, a purpose-built tender with cab protection was provided in 1965, entering service from 17 August. Still proudly showing off this acquisition and her new FR green livery, she rounds Whistling Curve, nearing the end of the climb to Tan-y-Bwlch, on Whit Monday, 30 May 1966, with the 1.10 p.m. train from Porthmadog. Behind are coach 15 and bowsiders, still in the green and cream livery applied since re-opening in 1955. ***Michael Mensing***

Inevitably, few railways can have all their vehicles in action all of the time. Most preserved lines have items of rolling stock await-ing time, labour and money to be lavished on them. In the Glan-y-mor yard of Boston Lodge, on 30 April 1966, on the site of part of the old paint shop, are, l-r, *Princess* under wraps, the cab of Fairlie *Taliesin/Earl of Merioneth*, *Welsh Pony* and the ex-Harrogate Gas Works Peckett locomotive. The latter, brought to the railway in 1957 as a reserve, was never used. Subsequently found to be unsuit-able, it was exchanged for a modern diesel. To the right, beyond the four slate wagons and perched on another pair, is the body of brake 3rd no.10, its bogies having been removed for use elsewhere. To the left of the line of engines, an extension to the original carriage shed has progressed as far as a steel frame awaiting cladding. Interestingly, *Princess* and *Welsh Pony* still await attention and the Peckett has been sold, whilst *Palmerston*, standing withdrawn and unsheeted by the sea at this time, has since been restored! *Eric Bareham*

As 1966 progressed, more coaches were re-liveried into the pseudo-teak finish. Here, in September, coach 23, newly rebuilt with full length doors and plywood replacing the original matchboarding, stands on a siding in Harbour station, in company with a static visitor. Having miraculously survived a long and tortuous history, K1, the World's first Garratt locomotive, was eventually bought by the FR and brought to Porthmadog, arriving at Harbour station in March 1966. In near-original lined-black livery, the historical importance of the engine was probably unknown to most visitors of the time, even to those who took photographs of it. Thankfully, it has been receiving much love and attention over the past few years and as the new century dawned, was well on the way to being reborn, to run on the rebuilt Welsh Highland Railway. *R C Riley*

17

Due to a number of factors, 1966 saw the first season for many without a double-Fairlie in operation. Slightly sick with problems in both tubes and fireboxes, *Merddin Emrys* languished in Boston Lodge Works, available only for emergencies, until the end of August, when he was returned to traffic for just two weeks. During that short period, he is seen at Harbour station, running round an afternoon arrival from Tan-y-Bwlch. The loco's lined-green livery, now nearly a decade old, looks very smart in the sunshine. After this brief burst of activity, having covered only 206 miles, Merddin disappeared into Boston Lodge once more, to reappear in 1970 looking rather different. *R C Riley*

FESTINIOG RAILWAY
FIRST CLASS FREE PASS
FROM ....
TO ....AND BACK
ISSUED TO
Mr. ....
A. G. W. GARRAWAY
General Manager
F76—Williamson, Ticket Printer, Ashton

0744

Whilst, during the 1960s, Tan-y-Bwlch was the end of the line to the general public, the railway was pressing ahead with work on the next stretch of line and giving attention to the achievement of the next extension. One problem structure in this phase, as regards clearances for both locomotives and coaching stock, was Garnedd Tunnel, on the ridge of the hill above Tan-y-Bwlch. Built in 1851 to replace a short stretch of line running round the outcrop, it is only 60 yds. long, but is very tight in width and has limited height clearance. Whilst indigenous engines would have no problem in negotiating the tunnel, newer additions and new builds had to be checked for precise tolerances. On 3 September 1966, *Blanche* has been to Coed y Bleddiau, unloading rail, chairs and sleepers ready for relaying prior to reopening to Dduallt and is slowly propelling the empty permanent way train back down the line, closely watched by crew and bystander. *R C Riley*

19

A September 1966 view of *Blanche* bringing in the first train of the day illustrates yet another phase in the development of Tan-y-Bwlch. Anticipating the needs of passengers at the soon-to-be-terminus at Dduallt, the railway built a refreshment kiosk and put it to temporary use at Tan-y-Bwlch in the interim; in deference to its wooden construction, it was soon nicknamed the 'Bunny Hutch'! The 1873-vintage station building, centre, has been given a coat of grey primer which, whilst protective, is hardly decorative; the varied carriage liveries could be said to fall into the same category. To the right, some light engineering work is being applied to an old railway vehicle frame. *R C Riley*

A look back at the 1959 view of *Taliesin* **at Tan-y-Bwlch -** on page 7 - will show what strides the railway has made at the station in the ensuing decade. In this view from September 1968 the hillsides in the background may still be treeless, but in the foreground, previous sidings to the goods shed have been removed and 'sheep grazing' has disappeared. Changing perceptions of safe practice, coupled with greatly increased traffic, caused fencing to be erected to preclude passengers wandering about the site. *Blanche* waits with a down train, formed of stock in the new varnished livery, with the exception of van no.2, an ex-quarrymen's coach of 1885, temporarily in use pending the completion of Observation Car 101. The older vehicles of the second train set, however, seen in the distance on the Up line by the 1873 station building, still bear green and ivory livery. Following the opening of the extension to Dduallt a few months earlier, on 6 April 1968, Tan-y-Bwlch ceased to be the northern terminus, becoming instead an essential crossing point. *Howard Wilson*

(Left) Another new addition to the locomotive roster came in the form of *Mountaineer*, acquired by Society Director John Ransom and donated to the railway in 1967. Originally built in the USA in 1917 for service in France, the sheer bulk of the superstructure dwarfed fellow engines. This size immediately caused some problems and more than one amendment was subsequently made to its profile and general design. In September 1969, the cab has already been altered to fit the loading gauge, but this would see further attention during the winter of 1982. A service to Dduallt waits to leave Harbour station in the early afternoon sunshine. *Howard Wilson*

(Below) Having made the journey back to Dduallt, the railway then faced a major problem. The former route to Tanygrisiau and eventually Blaenau Ffestiniog had been flooded by the Ffestiniog Power Station scheme immediately north of Moelwyn tunnel. Denied this access to the next goal of Tanygrisiau, the only real solution was to raise the line above the lake high water level. Various schemes were considered, but all would need to climb quickly from Dduallt station. Gerald Fox came up with the answer and the 'Deviationists' did the rest, creating the spiral we see today, utilising stone blasted from the hillside to create the climbing trackbed. This is the view in May 1969, just to the west of the station site, with temporary rails laid on part of the new trackbed. Midge site is seen from Dingle site before the two were joined. *Howard Wilson*

TO
BLAENAU
FFESTINIOG

OLD
ROUTE

THE
DEVIATION

DDUALLT
STATION

FROM
TAN Y BWLCH,
PORTHMADOG

THE 1970's

As mentioned earlier, the rebuilt *Merddin Emrys* emerged from Boston Lodge for the 1970 season with a somewhat different appearance. Gone were the old graceful, rounded lines, as the fitting of the brand new parallel boiler had been accompanied by unusual D-shaped smokeboxes and square, welded, water tanks. These changes were only relieved by giving the cleaners and fireman the early morning duty of polishing the domes, a completely novel feature never before carried by this locomotive. *Merddin's* starker appearance can be well judged from this view on the approaches to Tan-y-Bwlch, in August 1971, as a train of mixed, cherry-red liveried stock heads north. ***John Edgington***

(23708)   (23708)
British Railways Board (M)
0041
SUPPLEMENTARY TICKET
CHEAP DAY (TOUR C)
VALID FOR ONE JOURNEY ONLY
Portmadoc Harbour to
TAN-Y-BWLCH
by Ffestiniog Railway
For conditions see over
0041

By comparison to the 'new' lines of *Merddin Emrys* seen in the last view, the traditional double-Fairlie design was far more pleasing. The appeal is evident here, as *Earl of Merioneth* rounds the Pen Cob curve in June 1972, accelerating away from Porthmadog with a morning train bound for Dduallt. Note the ample, but somewhat precariously perched supply of coal. The introduction of oil-firing from the early-1970s rendered this feature redundant. *Bryan Hicks*

PEN COB

24

PENRHYN CROSSING

In the course of its thirteen mile route, the FR runs through and by a rich variety of scenery, from sea level at Porthmadog, through woodland and along hillsides, to threading between houses and even crossing roads, as seen here at Penrhyndeudraeth. In July 1972, *Mountaineer*, in its first year of oil-firing, leaves for Tan-y-Bwlch, cautiously crossing the A4085, protected from road traffic by traditional-style gates.

Bryan Hicks

Another view of Mountaineer on the same day in July 1972, this time at Harbour station, arriving with the return service from the above view. Britannia Foundry, so long a feature of the entrance to Porthmadog from the Cob and giving employment to the area since the 1830s, although still standing, had been closed since 1965. Sadly, a purchaser could not be found to re-use the buildings; the Inland Revenue building that now occupies the site certainly does not share the architectural merit! Note that the previous fencing to the right has been taken away.

Bryan Hicks

HARBOUR
STATION

The date is 3 September 1972 and safety considerations are again in evidence, with a fence erected to keep humans from moving parts! *Linda* shunts coaching stock ready for an early afternoon departure, with ex-WHR coach no. 23 at the head, followed by no. 16 and bowsiders. In the early days after conversion to oil-firing, Linda's front end suffered badly from overheating. Until a heat-resistant black paint was found, both hers and *Mountaineer's* smokebox and chimney were painted aluminium, which weathered off to black very rapidly.

Geoff King

(Above) Despite its isolated nature, Dduallt station is still popular with photographers, but those that do take out their cameras here do not normally view from this vantage point. On 6 September 1972, during the period of Dduallt being the northern terminus, *Merddin Emrys* pauses before heading once more for Tan-y-Bwlch. The years since this view have very largely disguised the hillside in the distance, the vegetation growth, due to sheep now being excluded from the enclosed area, making it less conducive to a casual stroll! *Geoff King*

(Opposite page) As work progressed on the new alignment away from Dduallt, interest grew among enthusiasts and the public, to the extent that the railway ran some trains around the spiral as far as possible to the 'head of steel' workings. On 7 July 1973, *Merddin Emrys* stands by a temporary sleeper platform at Barn Cutting, the occasion of an open day for local councillors, etc., to enable them to view progress on the deviation - and to canvass their support! The bridge in the background spans the track from Tan-y-Bwlch. *Gerald Adams*

(Left) Having blasted through cuttings, to take the line 35ft. above the previous alignment beyond Dduallt, the railway literally came up against a blank wall of rock. A new Moelwyn tunnel was needed and some of the extent of the works required can be judged from this scene. Towards the end of 1975 a works train of rock spoil is negotiated out of the south tunnel mouth, on the somewhat primitive track laid as a temporary railway. It is perhaps fortunate that these endeavours were undertaken and completed before the present-day demands of the Health & Safety Executive, although the H&S mining inspectorate did have their input! *Albert Sell*

THE "DEVIATIONISTS"

There are those who doubt the efficacy of employing young people on the railway. The Ffestiniog, however, has shown that, under proper supervision, they can be an invaluable asset and that, with their enthusiasm thus fired, time spent is an investment for the future. This view from the spring of 1976 shows that the present-day awareness of their value is not new, with the three captured on the spoil wagon looking totally at home as their transport rolls gently away from the tunnel mouth to Moelwyn Siding. The excavator is parked on the site of one of the old inclines. *Albert Sell*

Breakthrough in Moelwyn tunnel, 294 yds long, came at 11.15 a.m., 1 May 1976. The following summer and winter months were spent perfecting the bore and fitting a concrete lining. Thereafter, track was laid to a point overlooking Llyn Ystradau, the reservoir that had flooded the original trackbed. The route of this latter can just be made out crossing the middle of the view from left to right (the right-hand half under water still, even at this low level), on 19 July 1977, as *Blanche* has run round her train at the temporary terminus. Officially opened just eleven days earlier and standing 600' above sea level, it gave passengers a grandstand view of the waters. The site of the original Tanygrisiau station can just be seen beyond the reservoir wall, directly above the second coach of Blanche's train.

R C Riley

31

Tanygrisiau station on 18 September 1979, yet another a temporary terminus, during the final push to Blaenau Ffestiniog. Officially opened on 24 June 1978, the new station on the site is some 4' above original, due to the need to climb to the summit behind Llyn Ystradau power station and needed much work in moving yet more rock to accommodate the required alignment. All that remains of the original station is the goods shed, albeit half 'sunk' in relation to the new trackbed. Here, the new *Earl of Merioneth,* built by the railway in 1979 at Boston Lodge Works - the first Fairlie since 1911 - waits to start its journey back down the line, its rather angular outline heightened by this angle.

Tom Heavyside

TAN-Y-GRISIAU

In contrast with the frenetic activity being undertaken further south to eventually regain Tanygrisiau, the line to the north lay dormant. At Glan-y-pwll crossing in 1973, the gates remain closed to the railway - as they had been since 1956 - though the tracks are still in situ, ready for the day that trains return. They were lifted shortly after this view, however, it being nearly a decade before the line into Blaenau Ffestiniog was restored. In the background, the steep incline that once brought slate to the railway from Nidd y Gigfran Quarry can be seen. Now that the railway has reclaimed the territory, the crossing house seen here is being converted into a volunteer's hostel. *Albert Sell*

THE
1980's

Prince completely missed the 1970s. Withdrawn for overhaul in 1968, he languished in Boston Lodge until a group of retired engineers adopted him and completed the work as a volunteer exercise. He returned to traffic on 21 April 1980, with his traditional frame arrangement restored but still wearing the lined green livery adopted as standard in the late-1950s. Of greater significance was his conversion to oil-firing, though the smoke here appears more like that from a just-stoked coal fire! The tranquil appearance of Tanygrisiau, on 12 July 1980, belies the strenuous efforts being made to restore the line to Blaenau Ffestiniog - just over a mile away, but symbolically much further! *MJS*

The results of some of those efforts can be seen in this view of the emerging joint station with British Rail, taken in early 1982. The standard gauge tracks are to the left, whilst the forthcoming FR presence can be judged from the footbridge and the slightly raised ground running from it. To the right sits a school building, constructed on the site of the old FR/GWR exchange sidings, whilst beyond, the white bulk of The Queens Hotel overlooks the situation, as it has done since the days of the original FR. The only remaining vestige of the old layout is the stone retaining wall, left, alongside which ran the old alignment of the FR, before swinging towards Duffws station. The ex-GWR station sat just beyond the far right-hand bridge pillar. *Howard Wilson*

It is now the summer of 1982 and this view from Dorfil footbridge provides as interesting comparison to the last view. With crew comprising husband and wife Derek and Anne Evans, *Merddin Emrys* starts a service for Porthmadog away from the new terminus; the BR Conwy Valley branch line train, left, having made connection just a few minutes earlier. The FR platform is still rudimentary and a relatively temporary fence has been erected to prevent passengers straying onto BR metals. *Roy Needler*

Whilst the above goal was being worked towards, there was still a railway to run, passengers to be entertained. On 22 June 1981, *Merddin Emrys* makes an attractive picture, slowing for the Penrhyn road crossing, on an afternoon Tanygrisiau-Porthmadog service. Observation Car 101 leads, with nos. 120 and 103 immediately following and aluminium car 116 bringing up the rear. Note the old signal wiring gear on the wall at the end of the fence. ***Tom Heavyside***

A 'before and after' of the trackbed - or lack of it ! - immediately to the north of Tanygrisiau station. **(Right)** Seen immediately prior to restoration, the not insignificant gap left by the removal of the Dolrhedyn bridge is obvious. The structure was removed in 1957 by the local council, to improve road access between upper and lower Tanygrisiau. Agreeing to be responsible for rebuilding should it be necessary, they thought it unlikely at the time, as restoration of the railway had then only reached Minffordd and the power station scheme proposed to sever the line! bottom With the large chapel building still dominating the middle distance, the line is..................

continued - below,right

.......now back in place, with the new bridge installed with the help of EEC funding in 1980, (though to a slightly higher level than previously by mistake!). In July 1984, Earl of Merioneth heads away from the station on the last leg of the run to Blaenau Ffestiniog, seen in the distance. Since this view, the chapel has been demolished, opening up the vista. Though it seems remarkable from the perspective of these views, prior to 1900 the road actually crossed the railway on the level! Both: *Roy Needler*

ONWARDS TO BLAENAU...

A massively important day for the Ffestiniog Railway. Nothing, not even the dreadfully wet weather, could detract from the huge importance of 25 May 1982 in the annals of the FR. 150 years (and two days!) since the Act incorporating the Festiniog Railway Company was passed, a throng of people greeted the very first FR service train of the restoration period into the brand new Blaenau Ffestiniog station, headed by double-Fairlie *Earl of Merioneth*, complete with appropriately worded headboard. Unsurprisingly, this culmination of nearly thirty years' effort attracted enormous interest; there are bodies seemingly everywhere (and even an ambulance crew showing interest). The BR side of the station, right, had been opened with rather less attention a couple of months earlier. *Roy Needler*

Like many another new development, formal opening of the FR's Blaenau Ffestiniog station came some time after the actual event. A year after the last scene, on 30 April 1983, The Rt. Hon. George Thomas MP, Speaker of the House of Commons, (later Viscount Tonypandy) is seen with mayoral and other dignitaries at the station, having ridden up from Porthmadog on the special train, this time hauled by *Merddin Emrys*. The headboard quite clearly - and certainly affectionately - refers to his frequent cry to Members of Parliament. While some of the formal party await the return journey, FR Magazine Editors Peter Johnson (facing, with camera, right) and Dan Wilson (back to camera, right) record the scene for posterity; fireman Shaun Mcmahon concentrates on his duties. The departure south from the station was quite spectacular, being a race to the far bridge against a BR diesel multiple unit! Note the striking resemblance between Dr W R P George (fifth from right) and his famous uncle, David Lloyd George!

Howard Wilson

BLAENAU FFESTINIOG

By the time of this view, on 17 July 1983, the railway had settled into a routine with its new timetable for the extended journey. On the last stretch into Blaenau Ffestiniog, the railway passes the site of Stesion Fein, the FR station which formerly made a connection with the LNWR/LMS Conwy Valley line standard gauge station. This latter is still extant beyond the decorative brickwork, but no longer open to the public, its role taken by the new joint BR/FR station. *Linda* prepares to attack the last stretch of her long climb, with the 12.20 p.m. ex-Porthmadog train, with coaches 23 and 19 immediately behind and no. 100 bringing up the rear. ***Hugh Ballantyne***

**While work to rebuild the line to Blaenau occupied enormous time and effort, the
section already open and carrying passengers could not be neglected** - trains must run
and passengers must be carried. The Harbour station layout was amended, to accommodate the increased number and length of carriages required for more and more trains and
the 'WHR' spur, on the far right, was removed by the end of 1984. On 5 September of
that year, *Earl of Merioneth* basks in the early afternoon sunshine, before setting off to
negotiate the thirteen-mile climb to Blaenau Ffestiniog. The presence of a small museum
in the former goods shed is indicated by the old-style disc signal outside. **T*om Heavyside***

It is widely recognised that the FR, on its long uphill journey, passes through some of the most attractive scenery in North Wales. The upper reaches of the line are, in places, dwarfed by magnificent mountain slopes. In this June 1985 view, *Mountaineer* heads back towards Porthmadog along the still relatively new alignment, overlooking Llyn Ystradau, dominated by the Moelwyns. In a delightful view of all three past and present FR routes at this point, exposed due to the extremely low level of the reservoir, the 'causeway' in the foreground is the alignment to Tanygrisiau used between 1842 and 1956. The original 1836-1842 route (over the inclines) ran, left, along the edge of the lake, merging with the post-1842 alignment by the clump of trees on the far side of the water. *Roy Needler*

41

Coupled with the magnificent scenery, the railway presents photographers with highly attractive vantage points. This spot at Dduallt is a favourite, capturing trains against the dramatic backdrop of the Manods as they climb hard round the spiral, leaving the station for Tanygrisiau and Blaenau Ffestiniog. On 24 August 1985, *Blanche* looks to be in fine fettle as she gathers pace on her journey northwards, passing the down Whistle board. The semaphore to her left indicates the station she has just left.

Hugh Ballantyne

DESTINATION BLAENAU

THE 'MOUNTAIN PRINCE'

Though not as steep as the A4085 road, as this climbs from the valley floor to cross the railway on the level on its way to Beddgelert, the railway's gradient leaving Penrhyn station is still sufficient to require hard work from the locomotives. On 24 August 1987, *Earl of Merioneth* accelerates away with the northbound 'Mountain Prince' mid-morning service, bound for Blaenau Ffestiniog. Attractively framed by the trees, this is a view that is not often utilised by photographers; a railway supporter would have a superb view of affairs from the garden beyond. The train has a slightly unusual formation, as the second vehicle, a bugbox, would normally be found at the head of a train. No.16, here leading, had been hastily added at Porthmadog to cope with a heavy demand for seats.

Judi Stretton

A change of management in the mid-1980s, combined with a clearer appreciation of changing trends in what passengers desired, brought about various amendments, the most obvious of which was locomotive liveries. *Prince* was the first, in 1986, receiving, as seen here heading across the Cob away from Harbour station, on 16 October 1988, a rich red, lined livery, reminiscent of an earlier, Victorian style. The assembled photographers' interest is little more than polite, however, as their presence and attention was for the following train. This was the day on which double-Fairlie *Livingston Thompson*, (previously seen in this book as *Taliesin* and *Earl of Merioneth*, pre- and post-1961), was towed to Tan-y-Bwlch by 'younger brother' *Merddin Emrys*, for the formal handing over for preservation at the National Railway Museum in York. Note that Britannia Foundry has now disappeared, replaced by the rather utilitarian Inland Revenue structure, right.

Peter Treloar

THE 1990's

During the 1990s, ever on the look-out for visitor attractions, the FR began inviting 'foreign' locomotives to spend time on the railway. It has proved to be a popular tactic with visitors/enthusiasts, volunteers and owners/operators of those locomotives alike. In May 1990, before the trend was truly set in motion, however, near-neighbour *Russell*, from the Welsh Highland Railway base in Porthmadog, came for a brief holiday. It was not the first time that *Russell* had been to Harbour station, however, as he was a regular sight there until the mid-1930s, when the FR and WHR were physically linked by rails across Britannia Bridge, and had joined in the 1988 Gala. Seen here heading south from Minffordd, his size, compared to the standard FR loading gauge, is readily apparent. *Peter Treloar*

Volunteers are the life-blood of preserved railways. Many also enjoy the services of dedicated paid staff, but the count-less hours of enthusiastic 'free' labour are essential. Without such people the railway would never have been revived, let alone grow into the major tourist attraction it is today. As has been mentioned before, the Ffestiniog was one of the first to both recognise this importance and to engender enthusiasm amongst 'kids' of all ages, representing an investment for the future. The secret seems to be to combine responsibility with fun and a sense of achievement, for all to add their own colour to the railway - and not just with a paint pot! - and a special camaraderie often pertains. This motley crew - the 'Class of '93 - is seen gathered on Harbour station platform on 1st January of that year, waiting for their works train, with 'mother' Eileen Clayton, plus Sebastian, watching over matters.

Judi Stretton

BOSTON LODGE HALT

The train now arriving.... Now happily restored to his proper shape, resplendent in a highly attractive maroon coat and oil-fired, *Merddin Emrys* enters Boston Lodge Halt on a bright 29 July 1991, with 1445 ex-Blaenau Ffestiniog, with driver Arthur Brooks and guard preparing for the station stop. *MJS*

1993 saw the introduction of what has become an almost biennial feature, the May Day Bank Holiday Gala. The occasion for that year was the celebration of the centenary of the two 'ladies' - *Linda* and *Blanche*. The weekend programme was full of celebratory junketing and was blessed with superb weather. *Linda* was given a coat of new, blue paint and she and *Blanche* jointly stretched their legs, double-heading trains between Porthmadog and Blaenau Ffestiniog. On 2 May, they are seen restarting the 1200 ex-Blaenau Ffestiniog from Tanygrisiau - coaches full to overflowing, running some 40 minutes late due to slight operational problems and a delayed connection with BR. Throughout the three days, there were photographers aplenty and the whole event was voted an unqualified success. Note that the run-round loop at the station, seen in the shot of *Prince* in 1980, has been removed as an economy measure. **MJS**

Like *Prince*, fellow George England engine *Palmerston* was given a new look in the Nineties. Seen here framed by the flowers at Harbour station, on 7 July 1994, the new coat, applied the previous year to crown a long period of restoration, totally disguises the engine's 130+ years vintage, making it look brand new as heritage stock is shunted ready for a shuttle service to Tan-y-Bwlch. Near to 1890s condition, *Palmerston* - facing downhill in this view - is the closest FR locomotive to original condition, with original-sized tanks, cab and smokebox and still coal-burning, making an interesting comparison with oil-fired Prince. ***Tom Heavyside***

49

Two years on from that first Gala, the railway held another - 'All Our Yesterdays' - celebrating fifty years since V.E. Day and the ending of the second World War. The event was graced with the presence of three locomotives visiting from France and the railway was garbed in 'fatigues', with sandbags and mock gun emplacements at some locations. Again, the weekend enjoyed some good weather and the thousands of visitors, from both sides of the Channel, enjoyed the feast of events and presentations. On 6 May, Feldbahn 0-8-0 no.743, complete with French driver - here in conversation with David Black from the FR - prepares to operate the vintage shuttle between Minffordd yard and station, whilst *Castell Harlech* stands as a stationery exhibit, showing both the railway's non-steam side and the permanent way department's livery colours. ***MJS***

The history of the Cob, the mile-long causeway joining Boston Lodge to Harbour station, is fascinating and not without incident. The trials and tribulations in its construction, effectively taming the estuary, are legendary and some of the magnitude of that achievement can be appreciated in this view from above Boston Lodge Works, looking towards Porthmadog. At around 11 a.m. on a gloriously sunny 1 October 1995, *Palmerston*, now turned and facing Blaenau compared with the 1994 view above, assembles a Vintage Weekend slate train, watched by both visitors and Works staff. Due to hard work by many dedicated individuals, the FR has the largest collection of 19th century freight stock in the UK. Note how quiet the road is at this time of year, a far cry from the scene during the height of summer!

Peter Treloar

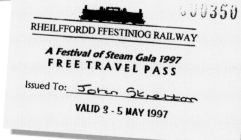

RHEILFFORDD FFESTINIOG RAILWAY

NP
National Power

105

ROVER TICKET
3ʳᵈ CLASS
THREE DAYS

Railffest99

Adult £30.00

NOT TRANSFERABLE
Issued subject to the Ffestiniog Railway Company's Bye-Laws and Conditions

1ˢᵗ, 2ⁿᵈ & 3ʳᵈ May 1999

000350

RHEILFFORDD FFESTINIOG RAILWAY

A Festival of Steam Gala 1997
FREE TRAVEL PASS

Issued To: John Skretton

VALID 3 - 5 MAY 1997

Thousands of photographs are taken of the outside of the locomotives and coaches and the vast majority of the visiting public go away only having seen the trains, the stations and the scenery. Few peer into the cabs and even fewer ever photograph the scene. If they did, they would see what confronts the driver and fireman as they prepare to take their passengers on their journeys, as here on the footplate of *Blanche*, seen on 24 August 1996.

Peter Treloar

TAN -Y- GRISIAU

As well as May Galas, the Vintage Weekend, originally set up by supporters of the railway's heritage to 'play trains', had, by the end of the century, become a feature in its own right, often held during October, giving an extension to the season and encouraging more people to return to the railway. On 26 October 1996, during such an event, *Blanche* double-heads with *Mountaineer*, about to restart the 1350 Porthmadog-Blaenau Ffestiniog train away from Tanygrisiau, made up of vintage stock. *Mountaineer* is here still in his 1995 Gala mock wartime livery, wearing no. 1265 and echoing the 1st World War origins and *Blanche* carries sand bucket and lamp to recreate her Penrhyn Quarry Railway heritage. The rails in the foreground are for a reinstated loop line at the station. ***MJS***

(Below) **The 1997 May Bank Holiday Gala did not enjoy the beneficial weather of its two predecessors**, much of the time being subjected to heavy rain or low cloud. Ironically, the sun came out on the morning after the last day, when most of the public had gone home and the railway set about returning to normality. As a 'jolly' and to thank the owners of the visiting engines, diminutive *Sea Lion* from Groundle Glen Railway, Patrick Keef's 0-4-0ST *Woto*, both coal fired and the FR's own *Conway Castle* set out 'to visit the quarries' at the top end of the line. They are seen arriving at Minffordd on their way up, the differing sizes being readily apparent. The sun was not to last even this day, however. Just a few moments after this shot, the clouds closed in and we had snow! The tree to the left, a long-time feature of photographs of the station, is alleged to have been planted as an acorn in the year the line opened in 1836.

Above-left) One feature of, especially, Vintage Weekends, has been the recreation of gravity slate trains. When constructed as a continuous railway, with the opening of the first Moelwyn tunnel in 1842, doing away with the previous inclines over the outcrop, the line had a constantly falling gradient. Horses would haul the empty slate wagons up the gradients from sea level at Porthmadog, with the returning full loads travelling down the 13-mile route under their own weight, slowed, if and when necessary, by hand brakes. Brakemen would travel at points along the consist, as seen in this recreation at Tan-y-Bwlch on 27 October 1996. *Linda* waits to continue the journey to Dduallt, where the wagons will be released. Long term volunteer Howard Wilson, in the last wagon of the train, nearest the camera in his trademark bowler, acts as flagman and senior brakeman.

Both: *Judi Stretton*

TAN
- Y -
BWLCH

Back again with Vintage Weekends and gravity trains. The length of train here is shorter than that seen above at Tan-y-Bwlch, in deference to the more aged and less powerful *Palmerston*. On 25 October 1997, the train starts out from its siding at Minffordd and approaches the station in the mid-morning sunshine, the number of brakemen being impressive but, perhaps, a little over the top! ***Tom Heavyside***

55

The end of the day in Boston Lodge yard - well, almost!. Unlike a car or even diesel locomotive, a steam engine cannot simply be 'switched off'. Though Ffestiniog locomotives' oil-burning fires can be 'shut down' instantly and there are no ashes to be thrown out of smoke or fireboxes, there is still much to be done before the crew can sign off. Mechanical parts must be checked and the motion cleaned of accumulated dirt and oil. The boiler is often 'blown down', to flush out sediment, and then refilled, ready for the next day. On 25 October 1997, *David Lloyd George's* driver, Peter Lawson, checks with his firewoman, Michelle Gamage (centre) and two cleaners, that all has been done before putting the loco 'to bed'. The chimneys have been covered, to reduce the stresses induced by cold air as the boiler cools overnight.

MJS

A gloriously sunny 18 April 1998 highlights a contrast in liveries divided by almost a century. Double-Fairlie *David Lloyd George* displays the muted, but elegant, colour and style of the late-Victorian era, while Funkey diesel *Vale of Ffestiniog*, recently refurbished with sponsorship from National Power, is a study in late-20th century 'corporate image'. By coincidence, the two locomotives also represent a century's development of Robert Fairlie's theories of articulation. Though one is steam and the other diesel, each is carried on flexible bogies, enabling far more powerful machines to haul heavier trains than comparable rigid locomotives. *Vale of Ffestiniog* was on its way to meet one of its 'big brothers', a standard gauge Class 59/2, also in these colours and visiting Blaenau on a railtour. After arrival at the terminus, the two locos stood side by side - little and large and an unmissable publicity opportunity!   *MJS*

Virtually whichever way you turn on the FR, there are attractive photographic opportunities, even with run-of-the-mill movements. Seen here arriving at Porthmadog with the 1510 ex-Blaenau Ffestiniog, on 15 August 1998, framed by colourful flowers and rolling green hills, *David Lloyd George* makes an attractive picture with its nine-coach load.
Peter Treloar

PORTHMADOG ARRIVAL

FESTINIOG RAILWAY
PORTMADOC to
PLAS HALT
FARE AS ADVERTISED
THIRD CLASS SINGLE
Issued subject to the Conditions contained in the Company's Notices Exhibited at their Premises.
0424
0424

On the following day, 16 August 1998, Tanygrisiau is seen once more, but from a very different angle. *Earl of Merioneth* here climbs the rising gradient past Llyn Ystradau and the power station, having left Tanygrisiau station, seen in the middle distance beyond the reservoir, with another Porthmadog-bound train. From this view, the magnificence of much of the line's surroundings is amply demonstrated, as is the dwarfing of the railway by the scenery at this end of the line. *Peter Treloar*

THE
MAGNIFICENCE
OF THE
MOELWYNS

FESTINIOG RAILWAY

FREE PASS

——

FIRST CLASS

One of the major events of recent times on the FR, was the birth of a new single-Fairlie. Long the dream of many of the railway's servants, especially among the Heritage Group, the recreation of the original *Taliesin*, virtually from scratch, has added a vital ingredient to the locomotive roster and once again has shown the abilities of the railway as workshop and builder. Immediately prior to naming by Bill Broadbent, ex-FR Director, the new *Taliesin*, in temporary unlined black livery, stands in Harbour yard on 1 May 1999. The importance of the event and the interest generated can be judged from the attendance on the station platform. Robert F Fairlie & George Percy Spooner would have been proud! *Peter Treloar*

An unabashed indulgence to end the book! Tammy Stretton was introduced to the FR in the early 1980s, taken on holiday to North Wales as a very young girl by her parents; closer contact and involvement began in 1989, with her becoming a regular volunteer from 1991. Like so many volunteers, she has thoroughly enjoyed her time on the railway, but, also, the organisation has not been ignorant of her involvement and commitment. To partly recognise this and as a 'Thank You', a special train was run on 29 August 1999 to celebrate her 21st birthday two days earlier, complete with appropriate headboard. Taking a break from the food and disco, Tammy poses with her *Prince* at Dduallt, as the sunset turns to night. *MJS*

AU REVOIR FFESTINIOG